American Pharoah

By Jon M. Fishman

AMAZING ATHLETES

Lerner Publications ◆ Minneapolis

Lerner Publications Company
A division of Lerner Publishing Group, Inc.
241 First Avenue North
Minneapolis, MN 55401 USA

For reading levels and more information, look up this title at www.lernerbooks.com.

Library of Congress Cataloging-in-Publication Data

The Cataloging-in-Publication Data for *American Pharoah* is on file at the Library of Congress.
ISBN 978-1-5124-0829-4 (lib. bdg.)
ISBN 978-1-5124-0830-0 (pbk.)
ISBN 978-1-5124-0831-7 (eb pdf)

Manufactured in the United States of America
1 – BP – 12/31/15

TABLE OF CONTENTS

American Pharoah takes the lead at the start of the 2015 Belmont Stakes.

MAKING HISTORY

American Pharoah surged ahead as the **starting gate** opened. He quickly moved past the other horses in the race to take the lead. Hooves thundered and fans cheered as the horses sped down the track.

American Pharoah and seven other horses were racing in the 2015 Belmont Stakes. The race was held in Elmont, New York, on June 6, 2015. American Pharoah had already won the Kentucky Derby and the Preakness Stakes that year. Along with the Belmont Stakes, these are the most important horse races in the United States. The three races make up the **Triple Crown**.

American Pharoah *(front right)* races down the track.

It had been 37 years since a horse named Affirmed won all three races. Since 1978, 13 horses had won the first two parts of the Triple Crown. But they all lost the Belmont. Could American Pharoah win the race and make history?

American Pharoah fought to stay ahead of the pack at the Belmont Stakes.

American Pharoah held onto the lead through most of the race. But other horses were right on his heels. Belmont is a longer race than the Kentucky Derby and the Preakness. The extra distance has caused problems for would-be Triple Crown winners in the past. Some fans feared American Pharoah would tire and slow down in the **final stretch**.

American Pharoah increases his lead in the final stretch.

American Pharoah wasn't slowing down. As they entered the final stretch, he moved ahead by two **lengths**. He kept adding distance between himself and the horse in second place. American Pharoah had a huge lead as he neared the finish line.

Fans cheer for American Pharoah after he won the Triple Crown.

The race announcer called the action as American Pharoah crossed the finish line: "The 37-year wait is over! American Pharoah is finally the one! American Pharoah has won the Triple Crown!"

Winning racehorses such as American Pharoah are worth a lot of money. Some people say he could be worth as much as $100 million.

American Pharoah was born in Lexington, Kentucky. The area is home to many horse farms.

A STAR IS BORN

On February 2, 2012, American Pharoah was born in Lexington, Kentucky. The **foal** came into the world at Stockplace Farm at about 11:15 p.m. The newborn horse had a faint white star on his forehead. There were no other markings on the reddish-brown **colt**.

Tom VanMeter owned Stockplace Farm. He thought the baby horse looked healthy. "It was a good-looking foal, but there was nothing out of the ordinary," VanMeter said. He didn't know that a special horse had just been born.

A horse named Littleprincessemma was American Pharoah's **dam**. His **sire** was named Pioneer of the Nile. In 2009, Pioneer of the Nile finished second at the Kentucky Derby.

Pioneer of the Nile *(below)* is the father of American Pharoah.

American Pharoah's **grandsire** was Empire Maker. Empire Maker won the Belmont Stakes in 2003. American Pharoah had good **bloodlines**. But there was no guarantee that he would become a top racer.

A few months after he was born, American Pharoah moved to a farm called Vinery, accompanied by Littleprincessemma. At Vinery, American Pharoah was **weaned**. He was separated from his mother. This can cause a lot of stress for a young horse. But American Pharoah handled the change well.

In 2003, a horse named Funny Cide won the Kentucky Derby and the Preakness Stakes. He was one victory from the Triple Crown. But American Pharoah's grandsire Empire Maker beat Funny Cide in the Belmont.

After being weaned, American Pharoah moved to Taylor Made Farm. A few months later, he went to McKathan Brothers Training Center near Ocala, Florida. Workers at the center began to **break** American Pharoah. They put a saddle on him for the first time. They also got him used to wearing a **bridle**.

Young racehorses must be trained to wear a bridle.

Once American Pharoah was broken, his racing training began. He ran with grace and energy. But he didn't know the proper way to run on a racetrack. "The first time we let him [run free on a racetrack], he went too fast," said J. B. McKathan. The McKathan brothers taught American Pharoah the proper way to **gallop** during a race. The horse learned when to run fast and when to save energy. He also got used to going into the starting gate.

The McKathans liked what they saw in American Pharoah. He was "a naturally talented horse" according to J. B. McKathan. American Pharoah would soon test those talents on the racetrack.

Bob Baffert is one of the most successful horse trainers in racing history.

RACING SCHOOL

In spring 2014, it was time for American Pharoah to get a new **trainer**. Bob Baffert had trained horses that won two of the three Triple Crown races. But he had never trained a horse that won all three. He thought American Pharoah had a chance.

Before long, Baffert felt the young horse was ready for his first race. On August 9, 2014, American Pharoah raced at Del Mar racetrack in California. He would be running in front of a cheering crowd for the first time. The sounds, the smells, and the other horses would all be

Fans cheer as horses leave the starting gate at the Del Mar racetrack.

new to American Pharoah. To keep him calm, Baffert put **blinkers** on the horse. Blinkers are meant to narrow a horse's field of vision and keep the horse focused on the race.

Blinkers go over a horse's head to limit the animal's vision.

The blinkers didn't work for American Pharoah. He jumped and pulled against his rope before the race. During the race, he got caught in a tight pack of other racers. He moved outside when he should have stayed inside. Near the end of the race, American Pharoah looked tired. He finished in fifth place.

American Pharoah's first race was a letdown. "If this is our best horse, it's going to be a long summer," said Baffert's wife, Jill. But Baffert knew the colt could do better. "It was just a bad first day of school," he said.

American Pharoah's name was chosen by a fan through a contest. The fan misspelled the word *pharaoh* as *pharoah*. A pharaoh is an ancient Egyptian ruler.

Baffert kept working with American Pharoah. In September, the colt was back for another race at Del Mar. This time, he didn't wear blinkers. Baffert put cotton in the horse's ears to block the noise of the crowd.

Baffert also wanted to make sure American Pharoah didn't get caught behind a pack of horses again. He told **jockey** Victor Espinoza to push the colt to take the lead early in the race.

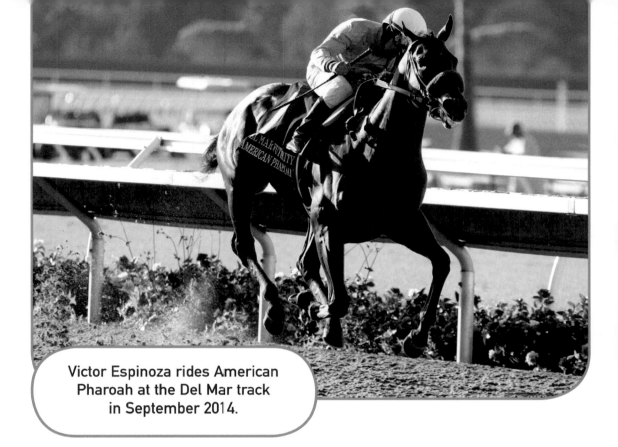

Victor Espinoza rides American Pharoah at the Del Mar track in September 2014.

That's just what he did. The horse streaked ahead of the pack. None of the other horses could catch him. American Pharoah stayed strong through the end and won the race.

American Pharoah won the FrontRunner Stakes at Santa Anita Park in September 2014.

RUN FOR THE ROSES

American Pharoah's first racing victory was the start of an incredible winning streak. He won his next race at Santa Anita Park in California. Then he won two races at Oaklawn in Hot Springs, Arkansas. American Pharoah blew away the competition in these four races. He won them by 22 lengths combined.

It was time for American Pharoah's biggest test yet. On May 2, 2015, he ran in the Kentucky Derby. The Kentucky Derby has been held each year since 1875. That makes it the longest-running sports event in the United States. Some of the top horses in the world race in the Kentucky Derby. American Pharoah was the favorite to win. Fans were impressed with his earlier victories and his smooth running style.

Rrring! At the sound of the bell, the horses burst out of the starting gate. Dortmund took the lead.

The Kentucky Derby is also called the Run for the Roses. The tradition started in 1896. Winner Ben Brush received white and pink roses after the race.

American Pharoah follows Firing Line *(second from right)* and Dortmund *(right)* in the 2015 Kentucky Derby.

Next came Firing Line and then American Pharoah. The top three horses stayed in that order as they zoomed around the track.

American Pharoah was still in third place when the horses reached the final curve in the track. As the jockeys leaned into the turn, Firing Line took the lead from Dortmund. Then American Pharoah made his move. He rushed ahead and passed both horses. He crossed the finish line about one length in front of Firing

Line. American Pharoah had won the Kentucky Derby! He was covered in roses in the **winner's circle** after the race.

Baffert gave all the credit to the horse. "This American Pharoah, he's just something," he said. "He makes a trainer really look good." Victor Espinoza said it more simply: "He's just an amazing horse."

Espinoza and American Pharoah celebrate in the winner's circle after their Kentucky Derby victory.

American Pharoah *(right)* competes in the 2015 Preakness Stakes.

"WHAT A HORSE"

With his win at the Kentucky Derby, American Pharoah had the first part of the Triple Crown. Next up was the Preakness Stakes. The Preakness always takes place on the third

Saturday in May in Maryland. American Pharoah had beaten 17 other horses to win the Kentucky Derby. But only eight horses raced at the Preakness on May 16, 2015.

During his Triple Crown races, American Pharoah's tail was shorter than usual. That's because another horse had chewed off much of the tail!

It had been a hot, sunny spring day. But just before the race started, the weather changed. The wind blew and thunder rumbled. Rain poured down in sheets. Fans in the stands ran for cover.

Water made the track slick. The horses splashed out of the starting gate. Some of them looked unsteady in the wet weather. Mr. Z took an early lead. But American Pharoah quickly caught him and moved ahead.

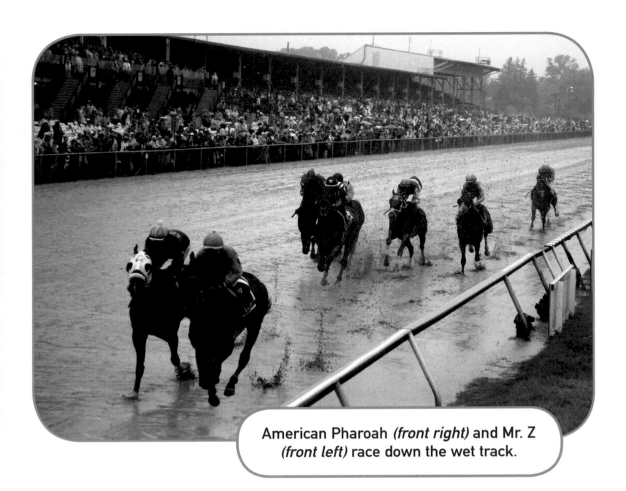

American Pharoah *(front right)* and Mr. Z *(front left)* race down the wet track.

Around the track they went. American
Pharoah and Mr. Z moved ahead of the pack.
As they came out of the first turn, American
Pharoah led by about two lengths. But then
Mr. Z and Dortmund began to close the gap.
Mr. Z got within half a length of the lead.

American Pharoah didn't let Mr. Z get any closer. With Espinoza urging him on, American Pharoah burst out of the final turn. He pushed ahead to make the lead more than two lengths. By the time he crossed the finish line, he was more than five lengths ahead. American Pharoah was the Preakness champion!

American Pharoah crosses the finish line to win the Preakness Stakes.

A few weeks later, American Pharoah won the Belmont Stakes and the Triple Crown. He became just the 12th Triple Crown winner in horse racing history. "This is the most exciting thing I've ever seen in my life," said former jockey Chris McCarron. "What a horse. What an incredible horse."

Espinoza waves to the crowd after he and American Pharoah won the Preakness Stakes.

Selected Career Highlights

June 6, 2015	Won the Belmont Stakes to complete the Triple Crown
May 16, 2015	Won the Preakness Stakes
May 2, 2015	Won the Kentucky Derby
April 11, 2015	Won the race at Oaklawn for his fourth straight victory
March 14, 2015	Won the race at Oaklawn
September 27, 2014	Won the race at Santa Anita Park
September 3, 2014	Won the race at Del Mar for his first victory
August 9, 2014	At Del Mar, American Pharoah raced for the first time and finished in fifth place
February 2, 2012	American Pharoah was born

Glossary

blinkers: pieces of leather that trainers put on the sides of horses' heads next to their eyes

bloodlines: a horse's close ancestors, such as its dam, sire, and grandsire

break: to train a horse to be ridden by people

bridle: gear that goes on a horse's head. The bridle is the bit that goes in a horse's mouth and the reins that attach to the bit.

colt: a male horse that is less than four years old

dam: a horse's mother

final stretch: the last straight part of a racetrack before the finish line

foal: a horse that is less than one year old

gallop: to run very fast

grandsire: the father of a horse's father

jockey: a person who rides a horse during a race

lengths: units of measurement that equal the length of a horse

sire: a horse's father

starting gate: a set of gates that open at the beginning of a horse race. The horses line up in the starting gate before the race.

trainer: a person who gets horses ready for races

Triple Crown: the name given to a group of three major horse races. The three races that make up the Triple Crown are the Kentucky Derby, the Preakness Stakes, and the Belmont Stakes.

weaned: when a horse is separated from its mother and taught to eat food other than milk

winner's circle: the place where the jockey and other people celebrate with the winning horse after a race

Further Reading & Websites

Amstel, Marsha. *The Horse-Riding Adventure of Sybil Ludington, Revolutionary War Messenger*. Minneapolis: Graphic Universe, 2012.

Donovan, Sandy. *Until the Cows Come Home: And Other Expressions about Animals*. Minneapolis: Lerner Publications, 2013.

Walter T. Foster. *Horses: Learn to Draw Step-by-Step*. Irvine, CA: Walter Foster, 2015.

Horse Racing Nation—American Pharoah
http://www.horseracingnation.com/horse/American_Pharoah#
Visit this website for photos, statistics, and interesting facts about the most recent Triple Crown winner.

Kentucky Derby
http://www.kentuckyderby.com
Stop by the official website of the Kentucky Derby to read about the history of the Run for the Roses and much more.

Sports Illustrated Kids
http://www.sikids.com
The *Sports Illustrated Kids* website covers all sports, including horse racing.

LERNER

SOURCE

Expand learning beyond the printed book. Download free, complementary educational resources for this book from our website, www.lernerresource.com.

Index

Photo Acknowledgments

The images in this book are used with the permission of: © Al Bello/Getty Images, p. 4; © Elsa/Getty Images, pp. 5, 6; AP Photo/Cal Sport Media, pp. 7, 17, 29; David Hahn/Icon Sportswire/Newscom, p. 8; © Aurora Photos/Alamy, p. 10; AP Photo/Garry Jones, p. 11; © Peter Cripps/Alamy, p. 13; © Jonathan Newton/The Washington Post/Getty Images, p. 15; © Horsephotos/Getty Images, pp. 16, 22, 23; © Cecilia Gustavsson/Getty Images, pp. 19, 20; © Jon Durr/Zuma Press/Corbis, pp. 24, 27; © Rob Carr/Getty Images, p. 26; AP Photo/Icon Sportswire, p. 28.

Front cover: Ray Stubblebine/Polaris/Newscom.

Main body text set in Caecilia LT Std 55 Roman 16/28.
Typeface provided by Adobe Systems.